Buster Books

The MAP

•COLOURING BOOK•

ILLUSTRATED BY NATALIE HUGHES

Edited by Bryony Jones and Jonny Marx

Designed by Jack Clucas

Cover design by John Bigwood

THE MAPS IN THIS BOOK:

World Map
Western Europe
Northern and Central Europe
Eastern Europe
Central Europe
Canada
North America
Central America
South America (x 2)
East Asia
Southeast Asia

North Asia
South Asia
Southwest Asia
Western Africa
Eastern Africa
Southern Africa
Australia
Oceania
Antarctica
Arctic
Flags of the World

First published in Great Britain in 2015 by Buster Books, an imprint of
Michael O'Mara Books Limited, 9 Lion Yard, Tremadoc Road, London SW4 7NQ

W www.busterbooks.co.uk f Buster Children's Books t @BusterBooks

ISBN: 978-1-78055-361-0

4 6 8 10 9 7 5

This book was printed in June 2016 by Ruho Corporation Sdn. Bhd., 334 Sungai Puyu, 13020 Butterworth, Penang, Malaysia.

WESTERN EUROPE

A guard at the Tower of London, UK

A jumper from the Shetland Isles, UK

Hiking in Luxembourg

Mont-Saint-Michel, an island monastery in France

Irish dancer

Tulips from the Netherlands

A windmill, Netherlands

REPUBLIC OF IRELAND

Dublin

NETHERLANDS

AMSTERDAM

UNITED KINGDOM

London

BELGIUM

BRUSSELS

GERMANY

Welsh dragon, UK

Statue of the Town Musicians of Bremen (based on a fairy tale), Germany

LUXEMBOURG

Luxembourg

PARIS

Roller skates were invented in Belgium.

FRANCE

The Tour de France, a famous French cycle race

BERN

SWITZERLAND

Houses in Bruges, Belgium

Playing an alpenhorn, Switzerland

A rooster, the symbol of France

Spanish Flamenco dancer

MONACO

ANDORRA LA VELLA

Château de Vianden, Luxembourg

PORTUGAL

SPAIN

ANDORRA

MONACO

Formula One racing in Monaco

MADRID

Winter sports, Andorra

LISBON

Luxury yacht in Monaco

Surfer, Portugal

Dom Luís I Bridge, Portugal

A tower of people, Spain

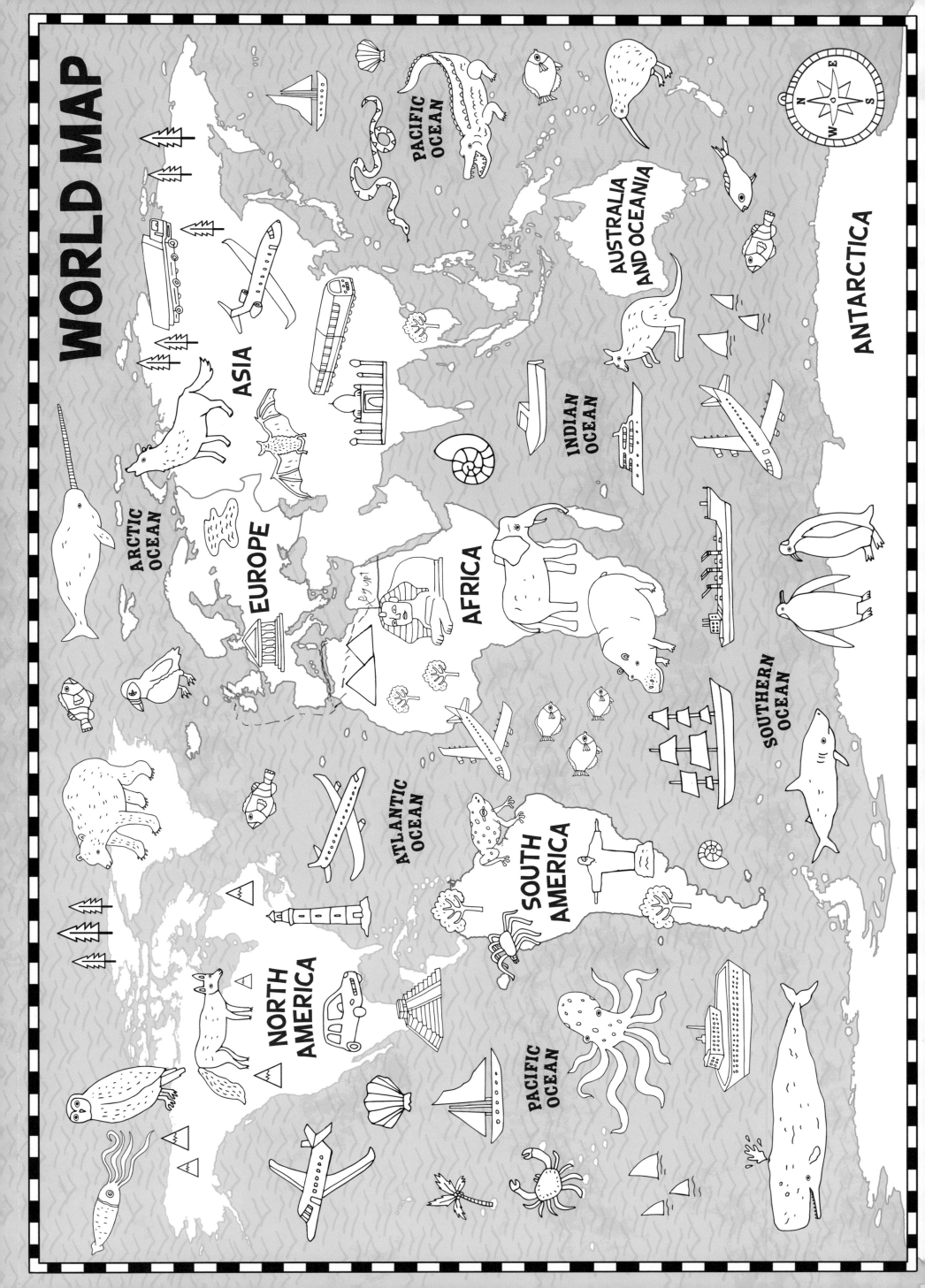

NORTHERN AND CENTRAL EUROPE

The Blue Lagoon spa, Iceland

A traditional Icelandic knit

ICELAND

Reykjavík

Iceland has a lot of volcanoes.

Puffins

Angler fish

Swedish orchids

A Finnish sauna

FINLAND

Elk

Windsurfing in Sweden

A viking boat

Rosemaling, a Norwegian decoration style

Sami people herd reindeer

A Latvian ballet dancer

SWEDEN

A viking

Traditional Swedish house

Heddal Stave Church, Norway

NORWAY

Midsummer maypole dance, Sweden

Oslo

Cross-country skiing

A Seto woman from Estonia

Helsinki

Herring

Stockholm

Tallinn

ESTONIA

LATVIA

Riga

A Norwegian troll

The Little Mermaid Statue, Denmark

Copenhagen

LITHUANIA

Ice fishing in Lithuania

Vilnius

DENMARK

A puppet from Czech Republic

Malbork Castle, Poland

Warsaw

An oriole, Latvia

A folk pattern from Lowicz, Poland

POLAND

Prague

CZECH REPUBLIC

Prague, Czech Republic

EASTERN EUROPE

Dracula, a fictional vampire from Romania

A dacha cottage in Belarus

European bison

Oină is a sport played in Romania.

A lynx from Kosovo

Mir Castle, Belarus

BELARUS

MINSK

Cossack dancers from Ukraine

Brightly painted eggs from Ukraine

Kiev Monastery of the Caves

KIEV

Przewalski's horse is a rare type of horse in Ukraine.

Alexander the Great was a Macedon king, born in Ancient Greece.

Vineyards in Moldova

UKRAINE

Sunflower fields in Moldova

The hills of Montenegro are great for trekking.

A Romanian health spa

MOLDOVA

CHIȘINĂU

Weightlifting is a traditional Bulgarian sport.

ROMANIA

BUCHAREST

MONTENEGRO

PRIŠTINA

PODGORICA

KOSOVO

SOFIA

BULGARIA

A valley full of roses in Bulgaria

Sturgeon live in the Black Sea.

SKOPJE

TIRANA

MACEDONIA

ALBANIA

The oldest gold jewellery ever found was at Varna in Bulgaria.

Brown bears live in the hills of Bulgaria and other countries.

GREECE

Ancient Greek vases

ATHENS

Albania has great beaches.

A windmill from Mykonos, Greece

The Parthenon in Athens

Greek fishing boat

Sveti Stefan is an island resort in Montenegro.

9

Wild pigs from Montenegro

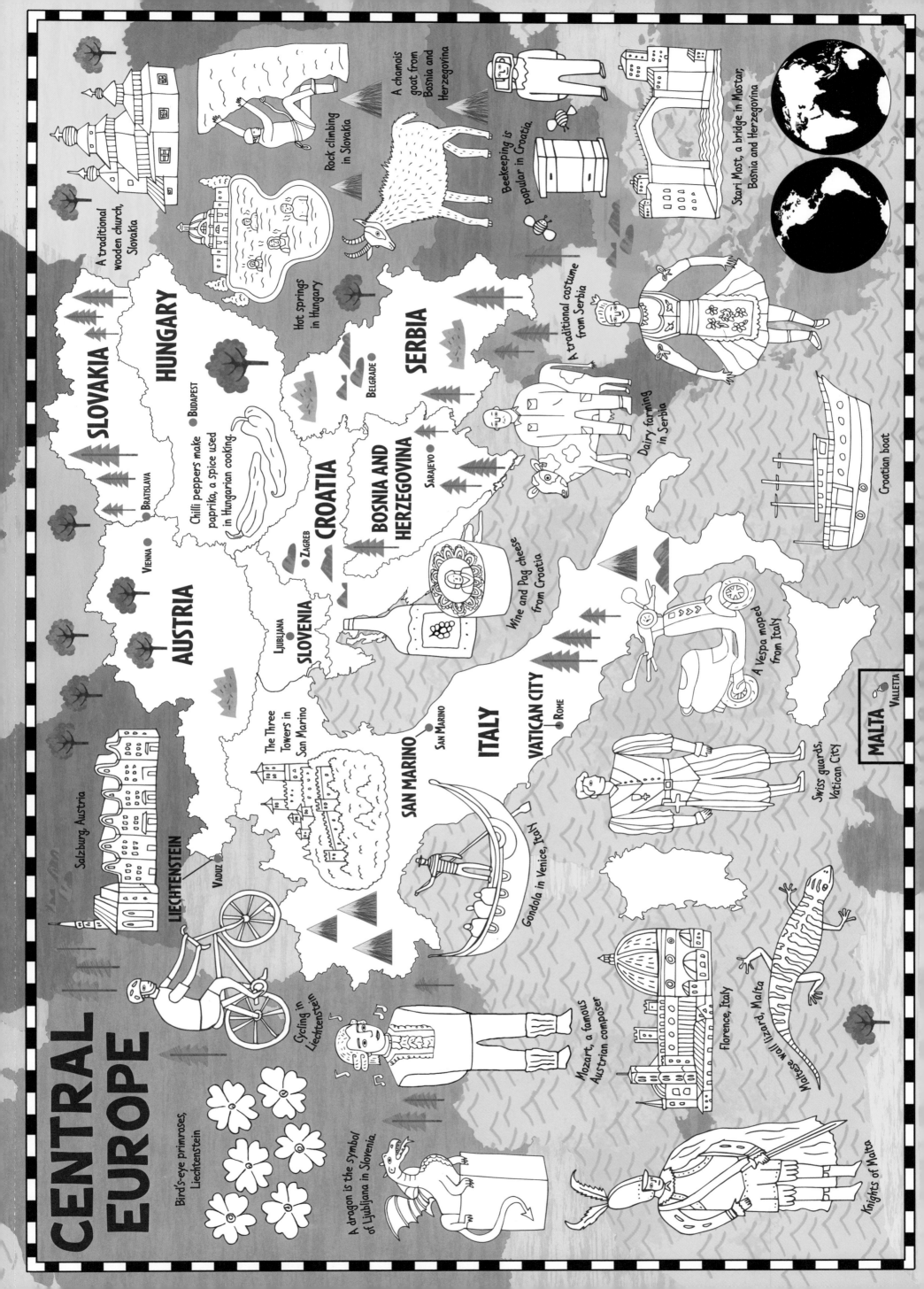

CENTRAL EUROPE

A traditional wooden church, Slovakia

Rock climbing in Slovakia

A chamois goat from Bosnia and Herzegovina

Beekeeping is popular in Croatia.

Stari Most, a bridge in Mostar, Bosnia and Herzegovina

Hot springs in Hungary

SLOVAKIA

HUNGARY
● BUDAPEST

Chilli peppers make paprika, a spice used in Hungarian cooking.

SERBIA
● BELGRADE

A traditional costume from Serbia

VIENNA ●

AUSTRIA

CROATIA
● ZAGREB

BOSNIA AND HERZEGOVINA
● SARAJEVO

Dairy farming in Serbia

Croatian boat

LJUBLJANA ●
SLOVENIA

Wine and Pag cheese from Croatia

A Vespa moped from Italy

Salzburg, Austria

The Three Towers in San Marino

SAN MARINO
SAN MARINO ●

ITALY

VATICAN CITY
● ROME

Swiss guards, Vatican City

LIECHTENSTEIN
VADUZ ●

MALTA
● VALLETTA

Cycling in Liechtenstein

Gondola in Venice, Italy

Bird's-eye primroses, Liechtenstein

A dragon is the symbol of Ljubljana in Slovenia.

Mozart, a famous Austrian composer

Florence, Italy

Maltese wall lizard, Malta

Knights of Malta

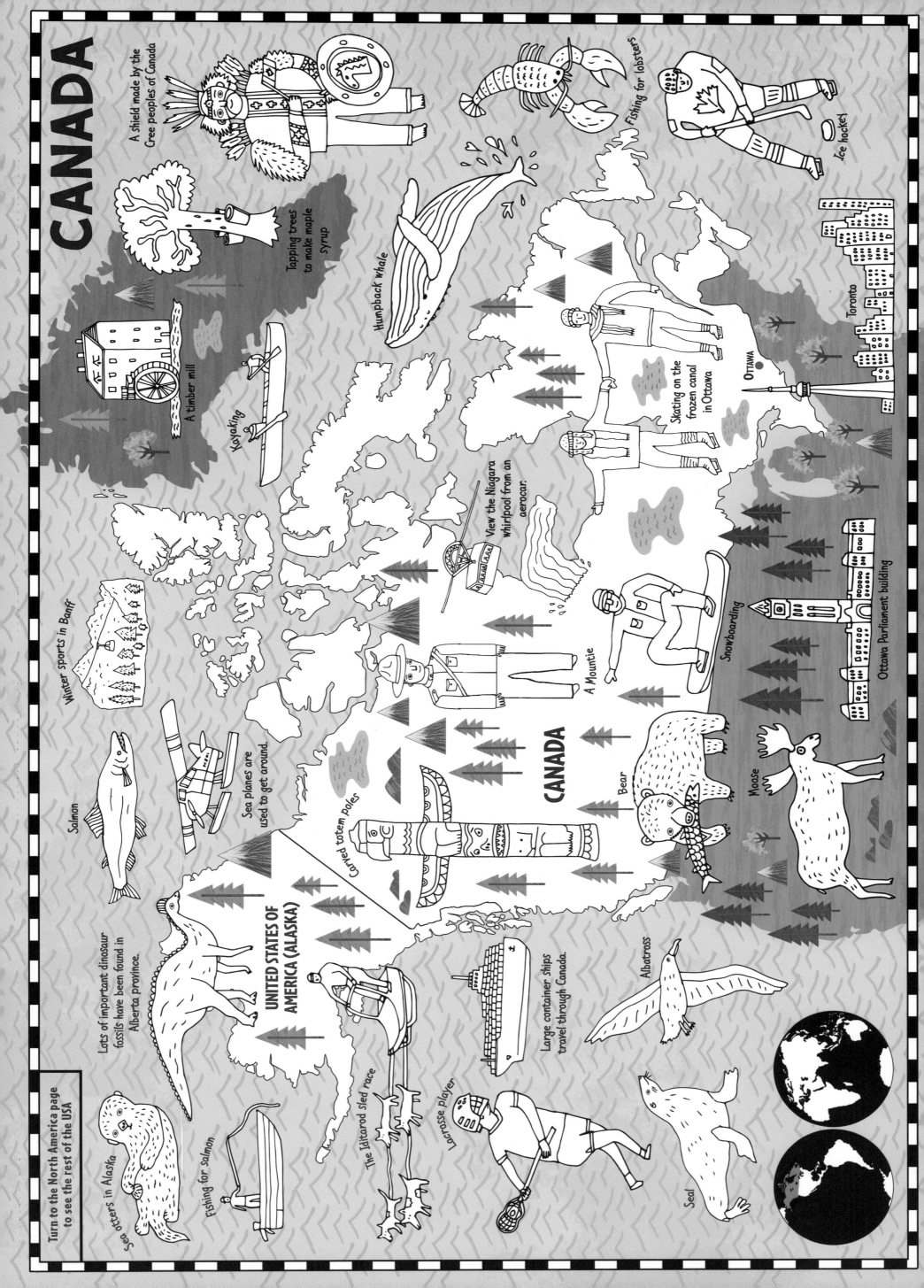

CANADA

A shield made by the Cree peoples of Canada

Tapping trees to make maple syrup

Fishing for lobsters

Ice hockey

A timber mill

Humpback whale

Kayaking

Toronto

OTTAWA

Skating on the frozen canal in Ottawa

Winter sports in Banff

View the Niagara whirlpool from an aerocar.

Snowboarding

Ottawa Parliament building

Salmon

Sea planes are used to get around.

A Mountie

CANADA

Bear

Moose

Carved totem poles

UNITED STATES OF AMERICA (ALASKA)

Lots of important dinosaur fossils have been found in Alberta province.

Large container ships travel through Canada.

Albatross

Fishing for Salmon

The Iditarod sled race

Lacrosse player

Seal

Sea otters in Alaska

Turn to the North America page to see the rest of the USA

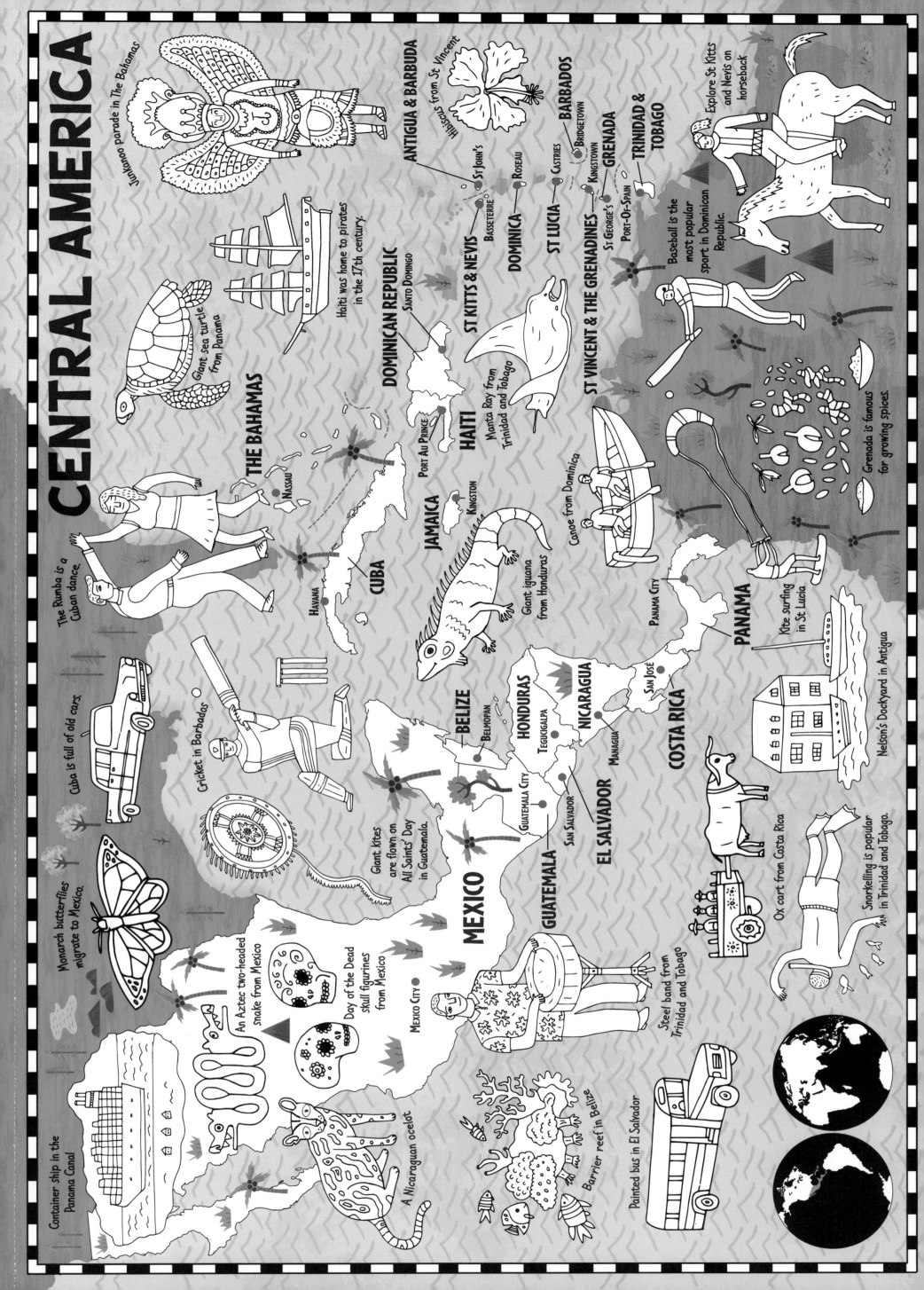

CENTRAL AMERICA

Junkanoo parade in The Bahamas.

Giant sea turtle from Panama

Haiti was home to pirates in the 17th century.

Hibiscus from St Vincent.

ANTIGUA & BARBUDA

St John's
Basseterre

ST KITTS & NEVIS

Roseau
DOMINICA

Castries
ST LUCIA

Bridgetown
BARBADOS

Kingstown
St George's
GRENADA

Port-Of-Spain
TRINIDAD & TOBAGO

ST VINCENT & THE GRENADINES

Explore St Kitts and Nevis on horseback

Baseball is the most popular sport in Dominican Republic.

DOMINICAN REPUBLIC
Santo Domingo

Manta Ray from Trinidad and Tobago

HAITI
Port Au Prince

Grenada is famous for growing spices.

THE BAHAMAS

Nassau

The Rumba is a Cuban dance.

Kingston
JAMAICA

Canoe from Dominica

Giant iguana from Honduras

CUBA

Havana

Cuba is full of old cars.

Monarch butterflies migrate to Mexico.

Cricket in Barbados

Kite surfing in St Lucia

PANAMA
Panama City

San José
COSTA RICA

Nelson's Dockyard in Antigua

BELIZE
Belmopan

HONDURAS
Tegucigalpa

NICARAGUA
Managua

Giant kites are flown on All Saints' Day in Guatemala.

Guatemala City
GUATEMALA

San Salvador
EL SALVADOR

Ox cart from Costa Rica

Snorkelling is popular in Trinidad and Tobago.

MEXICO
Mexico City

An Aztec two-headed snake from Mexico

Day of the Dead skull figurines from Mexico

A Nicaraguan ocelot

Container ship in the Panama Canal

Barrier reef in Belize

Painted bus in El Salvador

Steel band from Trinidad and Tobago

SOUTH AMERICA

Giant anteater, Guyana

Emeralds from Colombia

Handicraft shop in Colombia

Angel Falls, Venezuela

Venezuelan jaguar

Whale watching, Colombia

Armadillo, Guyana

CARACAS

VENEZUELA

COLOMBIA

GEORGETOWN

GUYANA

PARAMARIBO

SURINAME

BOGOTÁ

Maracas from Colombia

Vaquero (cowboy) at a ranch in Guyana

Capoeira, Brazil

Carnival in Brazil

BRAZIL

Rafting in Venezuela

Art from Suriname

Macaws in the rainforest, Suriname

Maracaibo houses on stilts, Venezuela

BRASÍLIA

Sugarloaf Mountain, Rio de Janeiro, Brazil

Ipanema Beach, Rio de Janeiro, Brazil

A gold mask in Bogotá Gold Museum, Colombia

Brazilian football player

Tapir, Venezuela

At the beach on Ilha Grande, Brazil

Climbing, Venezuela

Rhea, Brazil

SOUTH AMERICA

Woman in Quechua dress from Ecuador

Panama hat

Devil's Nose railway, Ecuador

Machu Picchu, Peru

Tarantula spider

Guarani peoples, Paraguay

Capybara

QUITO

ECUADOR

Las Peñas in Ecuador has lots of colourful buildings.

PERU

LIMA

Floating islands on Lake Titicaca, Peru

Gaucho, Uruguay

Iguazu Falls, Paraguay

LA PAZ

Llama, Bolivia

SUCRE

BOLIVIA

CHILE

PARAGUAY

Cusco, Peru

ASUNCIÓN

A monkey puzzle tree

Wine from Argentina

Rodeo, Chile

Parakeet

Darwin's frog

SANTIAGO

URUGUAY

Caiman

BUENOS AIRES

MONTEVIDEO

ARGENTINA

Stone heads from Easter Island

Buenos Aires, Argentina

Montevideo, Uruguay

Dancing the tango, Argentina

Trekking on a glacier, Argentina

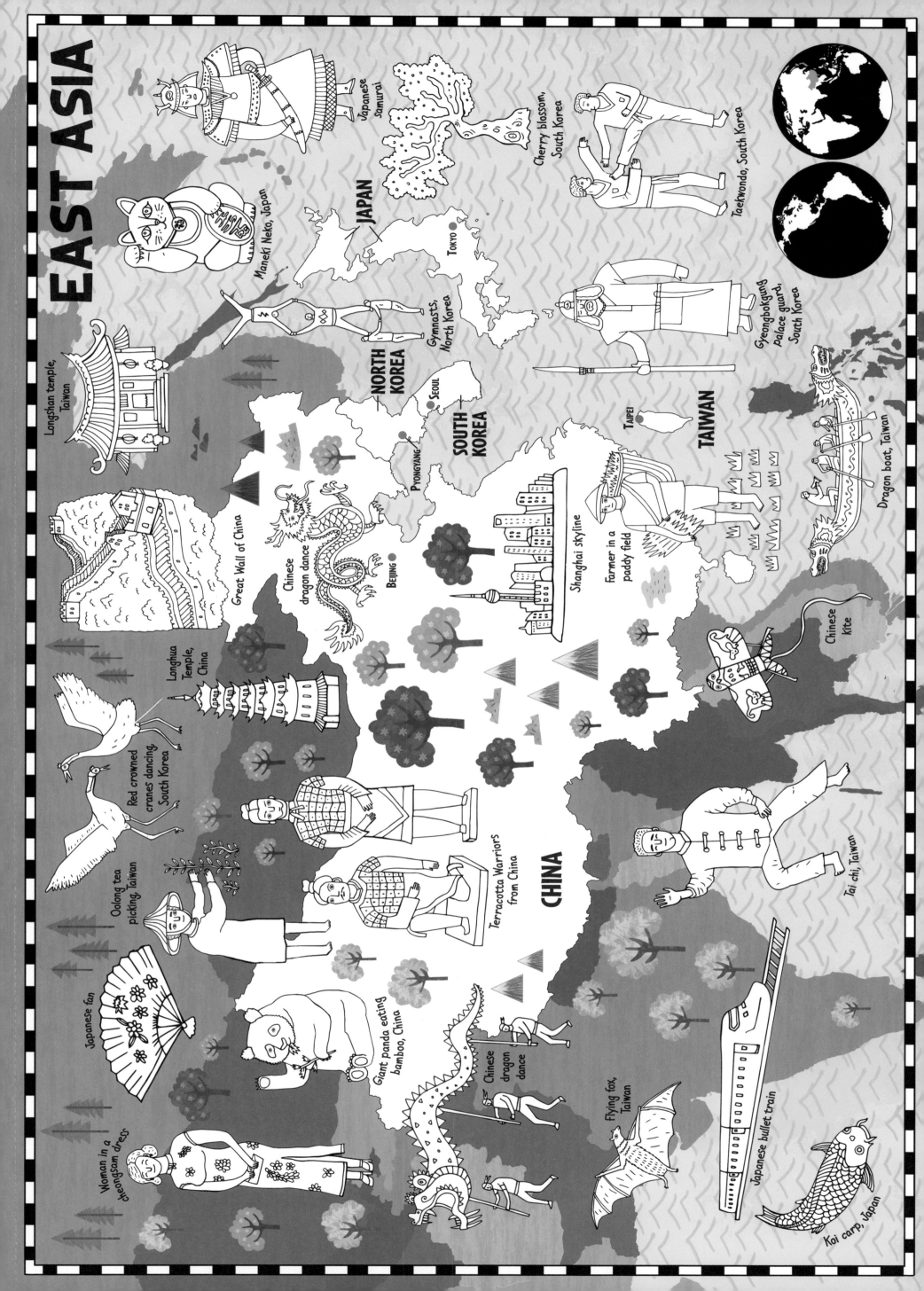

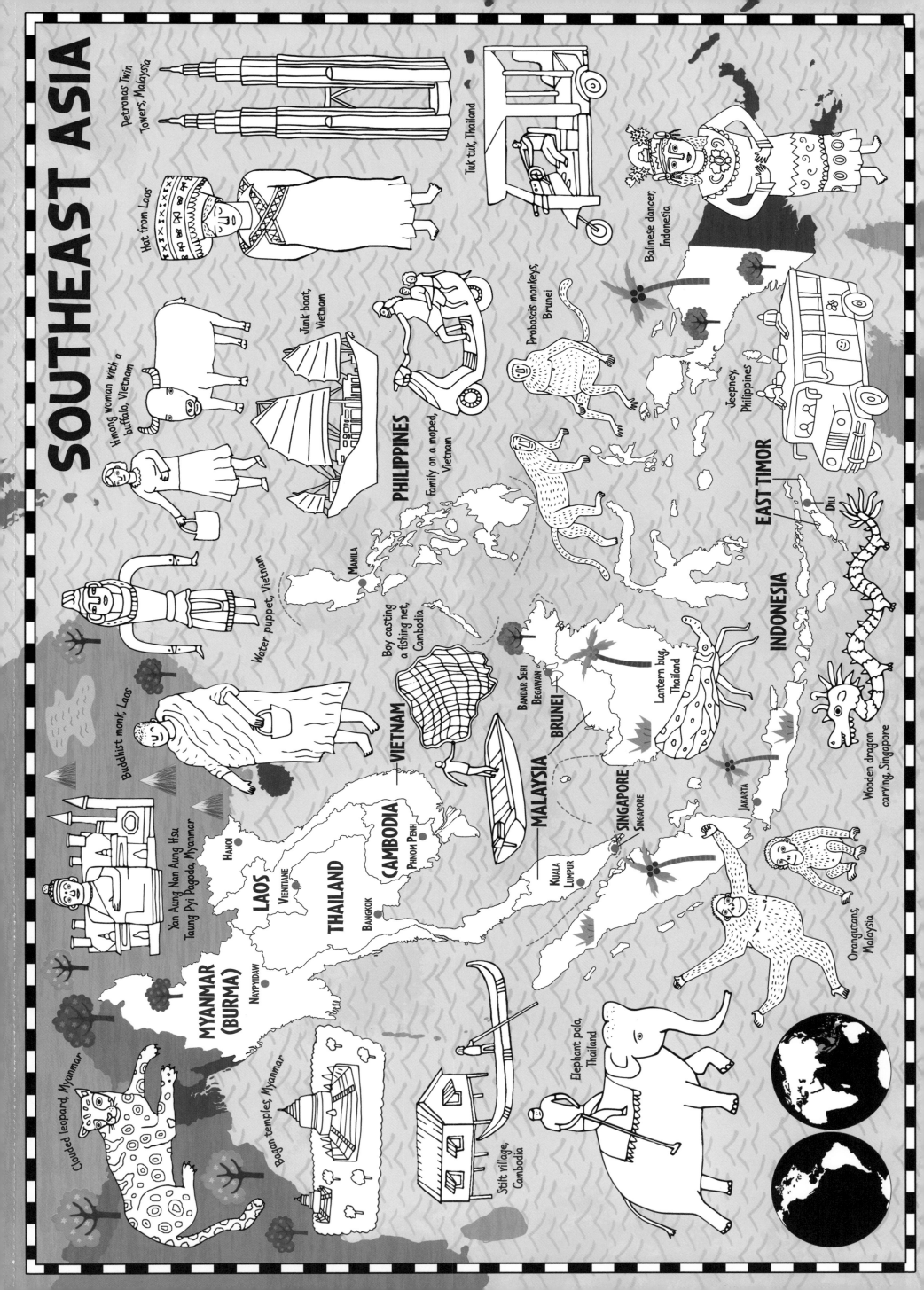

SOUTHEAST ASIA

Petronas Twin Towers, Malaysia

Hat from Laos

Tuk tuk, Thailand

Balinese dancer, Indonesia

Hmong woman with a buffalo, Vietnam

Junk boat, Vietnam

Proboscis monkeys, Brunei

Jeepney, Philippines

PHILIPPINES

Family on a moped, Vietnam

MANILA

EAST TIMOR

DILI

Water puppet, Vietnam

Boy casting a fishing net, Cambodia

Lantern bug, Thailand

INDONESIA

Buddhist monk, Laos

VIETNAM

BANDAR SERI BEGAWAN

BRUNEI

MALAYSIA

Wooden dragon carving, Singapore

Yan Aung Nan Aung Hsu Taung Pyi Pagoda, Myanmar

HANOI

CAMBODIA

PHNOM PENH

SINGAPORE

SINGAPORE

JAKARTA

LAOS

VIENTIANE

THAILAND

KUALA LUMPUR

Orangutans, Malaysia

MYANMAR (BURMA)

NAYPYIDAW

BANGKOK

Clouded leopard, Myanmar

Bagan temples, Myanmar

Stilt village, Cambodia

Elephant polo, Thailand

NORTH ASIA

Yak

The Nutcracker ballet, Russia

The Mongol rally, Mongolia

Genghis Khan, an historic ruler from Mongolia

Female archer, Mongolia

The Vostok I spaceship took the first man up to space.

Volcanoes of Kamchatka, Russia

Russian dolls

Siberian tiger

Milking a camel, Mongolia

Yurt

Patterned house in Baikalskoe, Russia

RUSSIA

MONGOLIA

● ULAN BATOR

Zenkov Cathedral, Kazakhstan

The Reclining Buddha of Ajina-Tepe, Tajikistan

Winter Palace of the Bogd Khan, Mongolia

Hunting with eagles, Kyrgyzstan

Tortoise, Turkmenistan

ASTANA ●

BISHKEK

KYRGYZSTAN

TASHKENT

TAJIKISTAN

St Basil's Cathedral, Russia

KAZAKHSTAN

DUSHANBE

UZBEKISTAN

TURKMENISTAN

ASHGABAT

Lion's Gate, Uzbekistan

● MOSCOW

Rug bazaar in Ashgabat, Turkmenistan

Traditional Turkmen costume

George Kourounis entered the Darvaza gas crater in Turkmenistan in a special protective suit.

SOUTH ASIA

Yeti, Nepal

Everest base camp, Nepal

Yak, Nepal

Golden langur, Bhutan

Water buffalo pulling a cart, Bangladesh

Edmund Hillary and Tenzing Norgay, the first people to climb Mount Everest

Archery, Bhutan

Bengal tiger

An Indian woman wearing a sari

Markhor, Afghanistan

THIMPHU

DHAKA

BHUTAN

BANGLADESH

Devil Dancing in Sri Lanka

Bicycle racing is popular in Sri Lanka.

KATHMANDU

NEPAL

Sitar player, Bangladesh

COLOMBO

SRI LANKA

SRI JAYAWARDENEPURA KOTTE

Stilt fisherman, Sri Lanka

Golden Temple, Amritsar, India

NEW DELHI

INDIA

MALÉ

MALDIVES

ISLAMABAD

PAKISTAN

KABUL

AFGHANISTAN

Flying kites, Afghanistan

Indus River Dolphin

Indian peacock

Indian elephant

Sea turtle, Maldives

Minaret of Jam, Afghanistan

Lotus flower, India

The Karakoram Highway, Pakistan

Kalash festivals, Pakistan

Indian cricket player

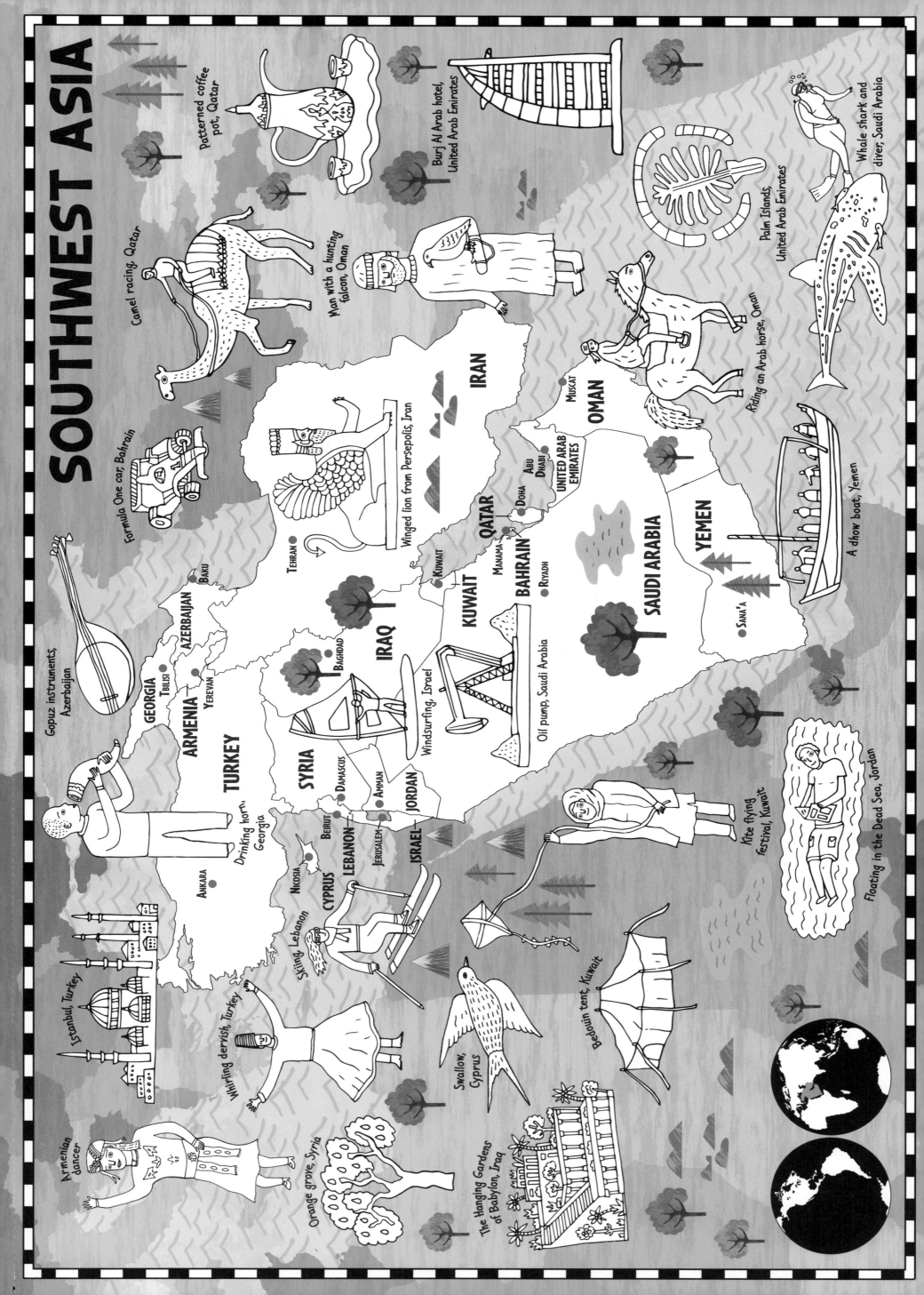

WESTERN AFRICA

Drummer, Liberia

Giant gecko, Cape Verde

Patterned tagine, Morocco

Glass lamp Morocco

Tunisian gate

Playing kharbaga (a boardgame), Mauritania

The Dakar rally, Senegal

Carpet from Ghardaïa, Algeria

Lucky hand symbol, Tunisia

Pico do Fogo volcano, Cape Verde

Martial eagle, Mauritania

Mamba from Guinea

Djenné Mosque in Timbuktu, Mali

Peanut truck, Senegal

Patterned sukhala house, Burkina Faso

Mask, Ivory Coast

Houses on stilts and canoe in Ganvie, Benin

Kora player, The Gambia

Emerald cuckoo, Sierra Leone

Ashanti gold, Ghana

Women selling goods at market, Ivory Coast

Triggerfish, Togo

Bijagós island dancer, Guinea-Bissau

MOROCCO — Rabat, Algiers

TUNISIA — Tunis

ALGERIA

MAURITANIA — Nouakchott

MALI — Bamako

CAPE VERDE — Praia

SENEGAL — Dakar

THE GAMBIA — Banjul

GUINEA-BISSAU — Bissau

GUINEA — Conakry

SIERRA LEONE — Freetown

LIBERIA — Monrovia

IVORY COAST — Yamoussoukro

BURKINA FASO — Ouagadougou

TOGO — Lomé

BENIN — Porto-Novo

GHANA — Accra

EASTERN AFRICA

Church of St George, Ethiopia

Camel caravan, Djibouti

Whirling dervish, Sudan

Windsurfer, Egypt

Snorkelling, Eritrea

Whale shark, Djibouti

Hargeisa market, Somalia

Maasai warrior, Kenya

DJIBOUTI
DJIBOUTI

SOMALIA
MOGADISHU

ETHIOPIA
ASMARA
ADDIS ABABA

Ethiopian coffee pot

ERITREA

KENYA
NAIROBI

UGANDA
KAMPALA

Batik fabric, Uganda

SUDAN
KHARTOUM

Ancient Kingdom of Kush, Sudan

SOUTH SUDAN
JUBA

EGYPT
CAIRO

Tutankhamun's mask, Egypt

Decorated shoes from Libya

Leopard, Chad

Butterflies, Central African Republic

CENTRAL AFRICAN REPUBLIC
BANGUI

Tea picking, Kenya

CHAD
N'DJAMENA

LIBYA
TRIPOLI

NIGER

Ostrich, Niger

NIGERIA
ABUJA

CAMEROON
YAOUNDÉ

Giraffe, South Sudan

EQUATORIAL GUINEA
MALABO

Tuareg people with goats, Libya

The Nigersaurus dinosaur was discovered in Niger.

NIAMEY

Women wearing traditional Nigerian fabric

African rock python, Equatorial Guinea

Mount Cameroon (a volcano)

Mountain gorilla, Uganda

Orchid, Cameroon

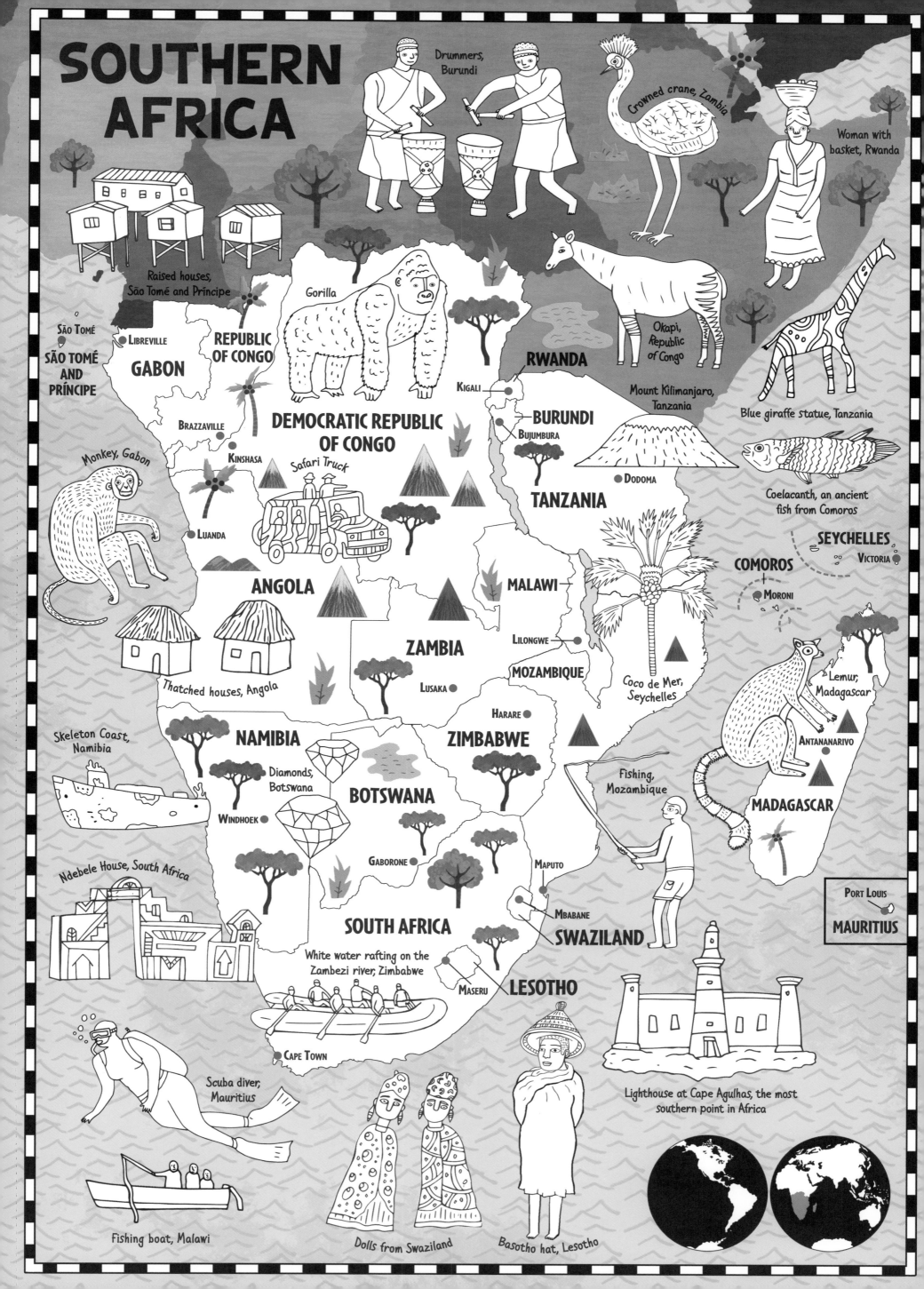

SOUTHERN AFRICA

Drummers, Burundi

Crowned crane, Zambia

Woman with basket, Rwanda

Raised houses, São Tomé and Príncipe

Gorilla

Okapi, Republic of Congo

SÃO TOMÉ
• LIBREVILLE

SÃO TOMÉ AND PRÍNCIPE

GABON

REPUBLIC OF CONGO

Mount Kilimanjaro, Tanzania

Blue giraffe statue, Tanzania

KIGALI •

RWANDA

DEMOCRATIC REPUBLIC OF CONGO

• BRAZZAVILLE

BURUNDI
BUJUMBURA •

Monkey, Gabon

• KINSHASA

Safari Truck

Coelacanth, an ancient fish from Comoros

• LUANDA

• DODOMA

TANZANIA

SEYCHELLES
• VICTORIA

ANGOLA

MALAWI

COMOROS
• MORONI

Thatched houses, Angola

ZAMBIA

• LILONGWE

Coco de Mer, Seychelles

Lemur, Madagascar

LUSAKA •

MOZAMBIQUE

Skeleton Coast, Namibia

NAMIBIA

HARARE •

ANTANANARIVO

Diamonds, Botswana

ZIMBABWE

Fishing, Mozambique

MADAGASCAR

WINDHOEK •

BOTSWANA

Ndebele House, South Africa

GABORONE •

MAPUTO •

PORT LOUIS

MAURITIUS

SOUTH AFRICA

MBABANE •

SWAZILAND

White water rafting on the Zambezi river, Zimbabwe

MASERU •

LESOTHO

• CAPE TOWN

Scuba diver, Mauritius

Lighthouse at Cape Agulhas, the most southern point in Africa

Fishing boat, Malawi

Dolls from Swaziland

Basotho hat, Lesotho

AUSTRALIA

The Daintree Rainforest is the oldest rainforest on the planet.

Aussie rules player

The Great Barrier Reef is the largest coral reef in the world.

Cape Byron Lighthouse

Tiger shark

Sydney Harbour Bridge

The HMS Endeavour brought an English explorer called James Cook to Australia in 1770.

Tasmanian devils are famously grumpy mammals that live on the island of Tasmania.

The beaches are great for surfing.

The Great Dividing Range

Sydney Opera House

Echidna

CANBERRA

Parliament House

Koala

Platypus

Wine region

Saltwater crocodile

Cassowary

Opal mining

Uluru (Ayers Rock)

AUSTRALIA

The Bungle Bungle Range

Much of the country is covered in sheep and cattle farms.

The Twelve Apostles are rock towers in the sea - but there are actually only eight. The rest have fallen down.

Diamond mines

Kangaroo

Great white shark

Didgeridoo

Aboriginal art

The redback spider is one of Australia's venomous spiders.

Australians are famous for their love of cricket.

The BBQ is a great Australian tradition.

Pearls

Most people in Australia live in cities, such as Perth.

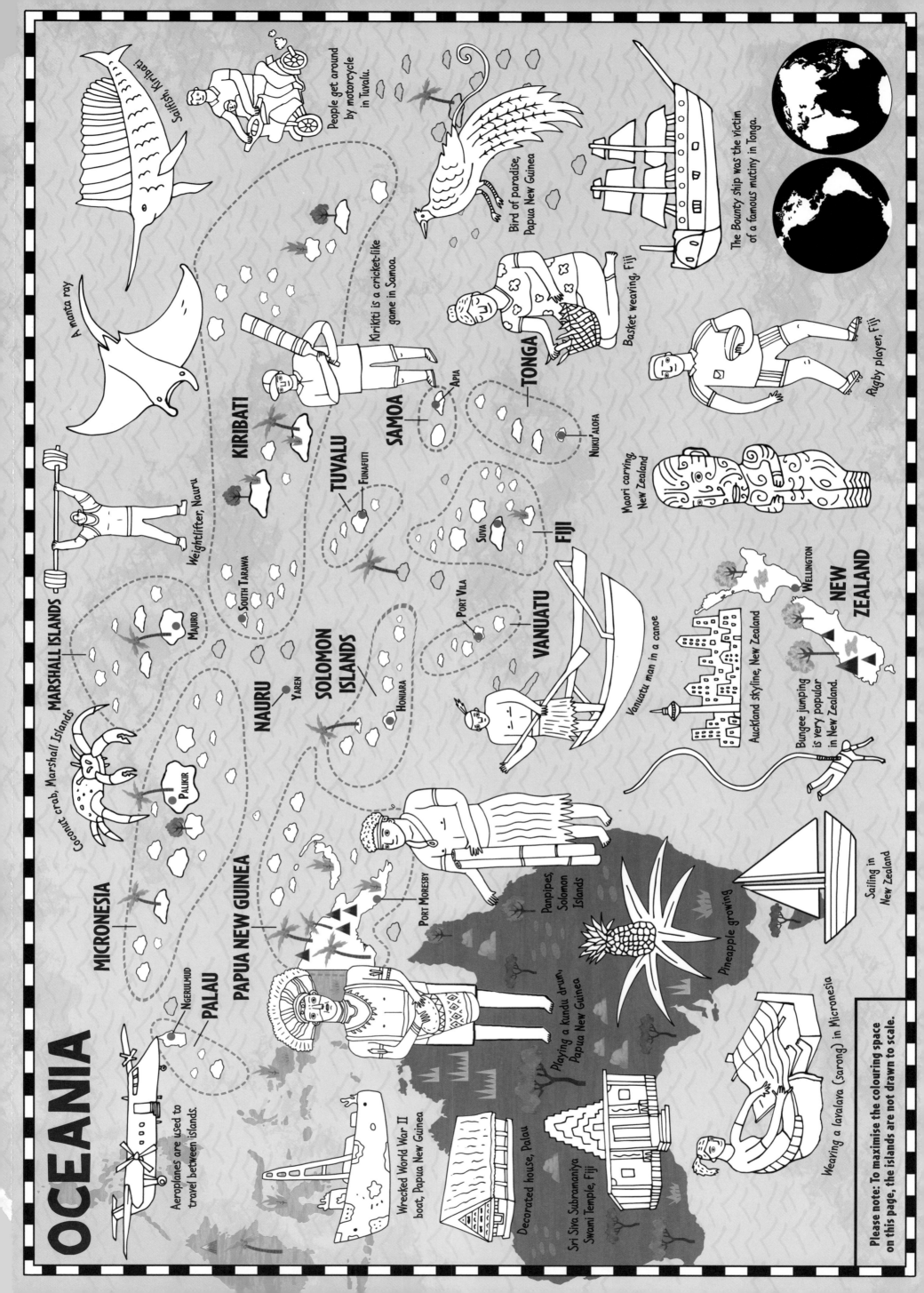

OCEANIA

Sailfish, Kiribati

A manta ray

People get around by motorcycle in Tuvalu.

Bird of paradise, Papua New Guinea

The Bounty ship was the victim of a famous mutiny in Tonga.

Basket weaving, Fiji

Kirikiti is a cricket-like game in Samoa.

KIRIBATI

TONGA

SAMOA

APIA

NUKU'ALOFA

Rugby player, Fiji

TUVALU

FUNAFUTI

Weightlifter, Nauru

SOUTH TARAWA

SUVA

FIJI

Maori carving, New Zealand

MARSHALL ISLANDS

MAJURO

PORT VILA

VANUATU

Vanuatu man in a canoe

WELLINGTON

NEW ZEALAND

NAURU

YAREN

SOLOMON ISLANDS

HONIARA

Auckland skyline, New Zealand

Bungee jumping is very popular in New Zealand.

Coconut crab, Marshall Islands

PALIKIR

MICRONESIA

PAPUA NEW GUINEA

PORT MORESBY

Panpipes, Solomon Islands

Pineapple growing

Sailing in New Zealand

NGERULMUD

PALAU

Aeroplanes are used to travel between islands.

Wrecked World War II boat, Papua New Guinea

Decorated house, Palau

Playing a kundu drum, Papua New Guinea

Sri Siva Subramaniya Swami Temple, Fiji

Weaving a lavalava (sarong) in Micronesia

Please note: To maximise the colouring space on this page, the islands are not drawn to scale.

ANTARCTICA

Humpback whale

Halley Research Station

People travel by plane in the Antarctic.

Leopard seal

Roald Amundsen was the first person to reach the South Pole.

Albatross

Tourists skiing

Research tents

Orca

Snowmobile

Icefish

Emperor penguins

ARCTIC

Arctic flowers blooming

Narwhal

Greenland village

Gyrfalcon

Caribou

Oil rig

Sami reindeer herder

Greenland costume

Arctic fox

Arctic gull

Arctic crocuses

Icebreaker ship

Yup'ik mask

Snowy owl

Dogs with sled

FLAGS OF THE WORLD
Colour in the flags the same shade as the coloured dots.

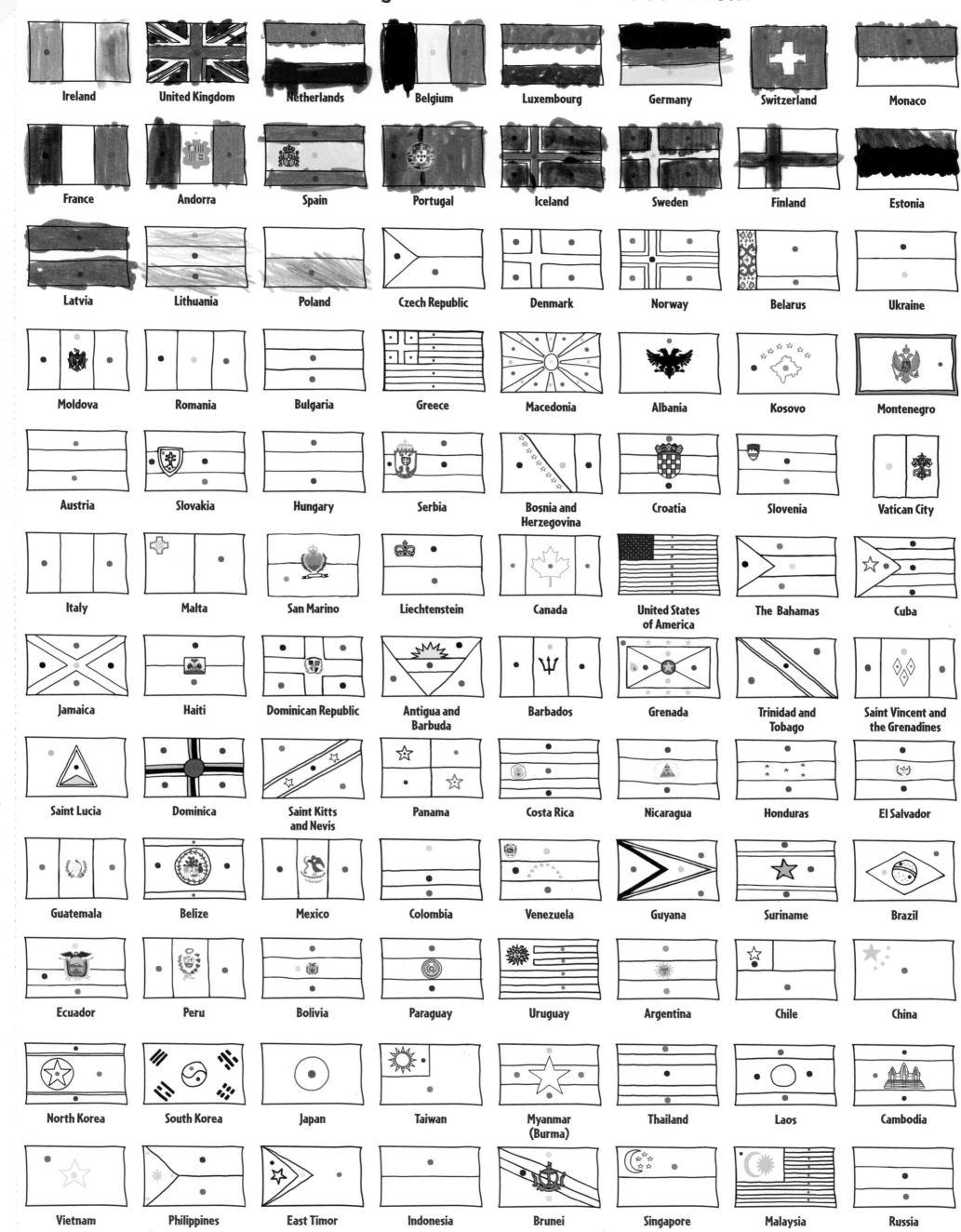

Ireland · United Kingdom · Netherlands · Belgium · Luxembourg · Germany · Switzerland · Monaco

France · Andorra · Spain · Portugal · Iceland · Sweden · Finland · Estonia

Latvia · Lithuania · Poland · Czech Republic · Denmark · Norway · Belarus · Ukraine

Moldova · Romania · Bulgaria · Greece · Macedonia · Albania · Kosovo · Montenegro

Austria · Slovakia · Hungary · Serbia · Bosnia and Herzegovina · Croatia · Slovenia · Vatican City

Italy · Malta · San Marino · Liechtenstein · Canada · United States of America · The Bahamas · Cuba

Jamaica · Haiti · Dominican Republic · Antigua and Barbuda · Barbados · Grenada · Trinidad and Tobago · Saint Vincent and the Grenadines

Saint Lucia · Dominica · Saint Kitts and Nevis · Panama · Costa Rica · Nicaragua · Honduras · El Salvador

Guatemala · Belize · Mexico · Colombia · Venezuela · Guyana · Suriname · Brazil

Ecuador · Peru · Bolivia · Paraguay · Uruguay · Argentina · Chile · China

North Korea · South Korea · Japan · Taiwan · Myanmar (Burma) · Thailand · Laos · Cambodia

Vietnam · Philippines · East Timor · Indonesia · Brunei · Singapore · Malaysia · Russia

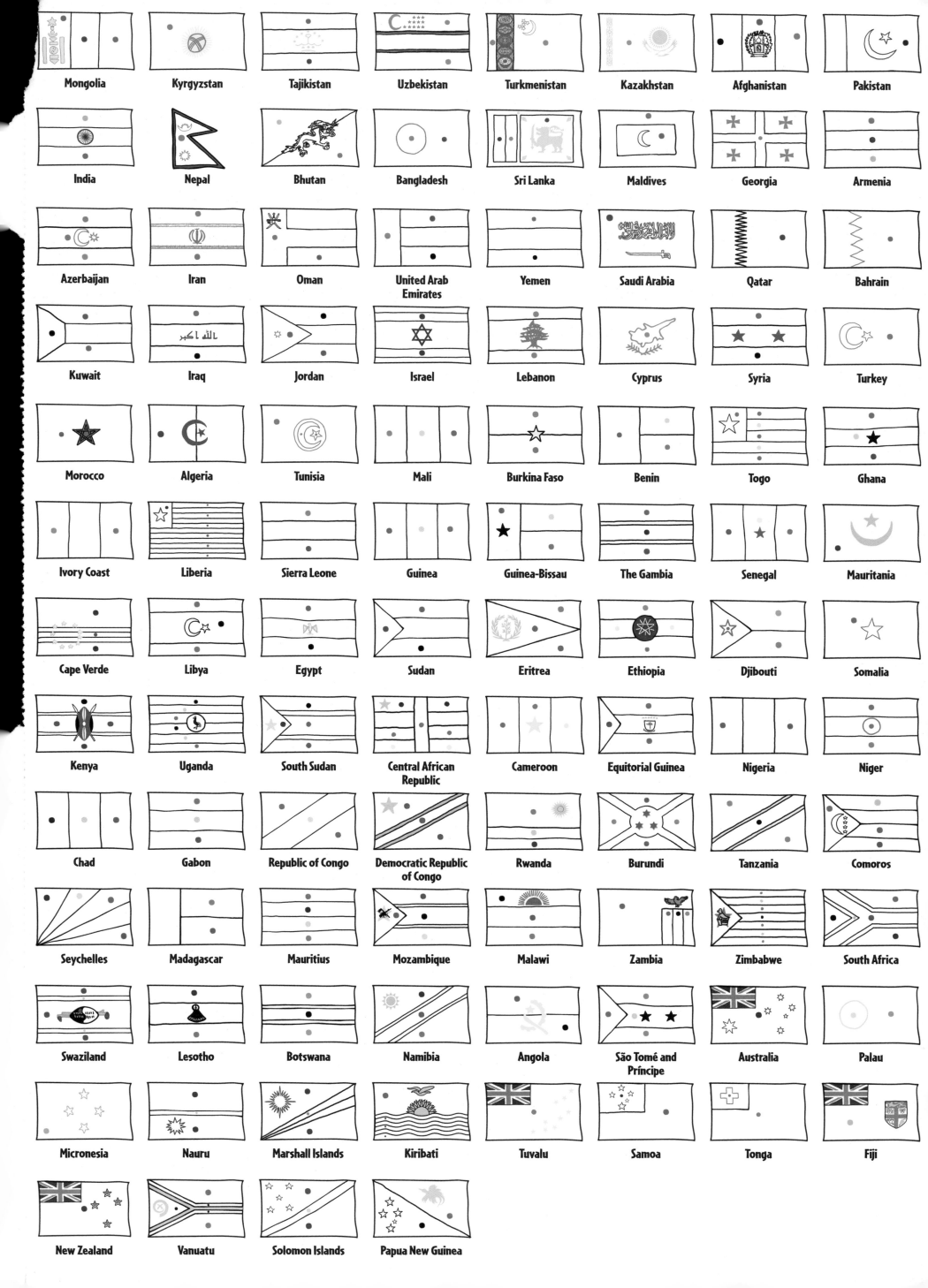

Mongolia	Kyrgyzstan	Tajikistan	Uzbekistan	Turkmenistan	Kazakhstan	Afghanistan	Pakistan
India	Nepal	Bhutan	Bangladesh	Sri Lanka	Maldives	Georgia	Armenia
Azerbaijan	Iran	Oman	United Arab Emirates	Yemen	Saudi Arabia	Qatar	Bahrain
Kuwait	Iraq	Jordan	Israel	Lebanon	Cyprus	Syria	Turkey
Morocco	Algeria	Tunisia	Mali	Burkina Faso	Benin	Togo	Ghana
Ivory Coast	Liberia	Sierra Leone	Guinea	Guinea-Bissau	The Gambia	Senegal	Mauritania
Cape Verde	Libya	Egypt	Sudan	Eritrea	Ethiopia	Djibouti	Somalia
Kenya	Uganda	South Sudan	Central African Republic	Cameroon	Equitorial Guinea	Nigeria	Niger
Chad	Gabon	Republic of Congo	Democratic Republic of Congo	Rwanda	Burundi	Tanzania	Comoros
Seychelles	Madagascar	Mauritius	Mozambique	Malawi	Zambia	Zimbabwe	South Africa
Swaziland	Lesotho	Botswana	Namibia	Angola	São Tomé and Príncipe	Australia	Palau
Micronesia	Nauru	Marshall Islands	Kiribati	Tuvalu	Samoa	Tonga	Fiji
New Zealand	Vanuatu	Solomon Islands	Papua New Guinea				